The Step-by-Step Way to Draw Fox

A Fun and Easy Drawing Book to Learn How to Draw

Foxes

By

Kristen Diaz.

License Notes

No part of this Book can be reproduced in any form or by any means including print, electronic, scanning or photocopying unless prior permission is granted by the author.

All ideas, suggestions and guidelines mentioned here are written for informative purposes. While the author has taken every possible step to ensure accuracy, all readers are advised to follow information at their own risk. The author cannot be held responsible for personal and/or commercial damages in case of misinterpreting and misunderstanding any part of this Book

Table of Contents

Introduction

Becoming a great artist requires creativity, patience and practice. These habits can flourish in children when they start to develop them at a young age. We believe our guide will teach your child the discipline and patience required to not just learn to draw well, but to use those qualities in everything they do. Your job as a parent is to work with your child and encourage them when stuck and feel like giving up.

The world of art is an amazing way for you and your child to communicate and bond. When you open this book and start to create with your little one, you will delight in the things you learn about them and they will feel closer to you. Your support and gentle suggestions will help them be more patient with themselves and soon they will take the time needed to create spectacular drawings of which you can both be proud.

This guide is useful for parents as it teaches fundamentals of drawing and simple techniques. By following this book with your child, adults will learn patience and develop their skills as a child's most important teacher. By spending a few hours together you will develop a strong connection and learn the best ways of communicating with each other. It is truly a rewarding experience when you and your child create a masterpiece by working together!

How to draw Fox1

1) Draw a fox head just above the center of the leaf for a round
top, pointed at the sides and slightly convex below.

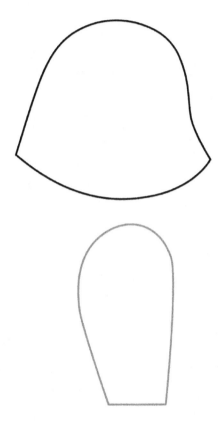

2) Add an elongated semi-oval below, as shown in the example.

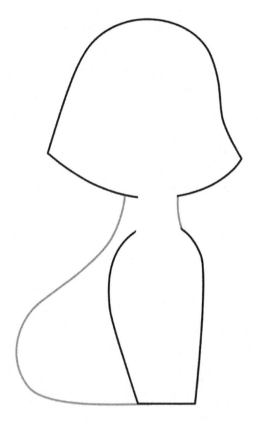

3) Connect the head and torso with a neck, add the back

of the torso with a large curved line.

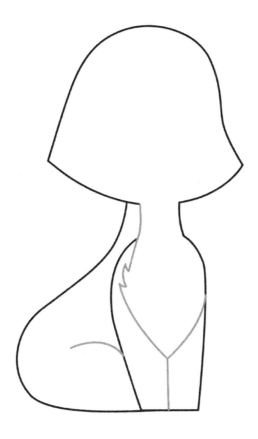

4) Draw chest and paws with the help of several lines,

be close to the original.

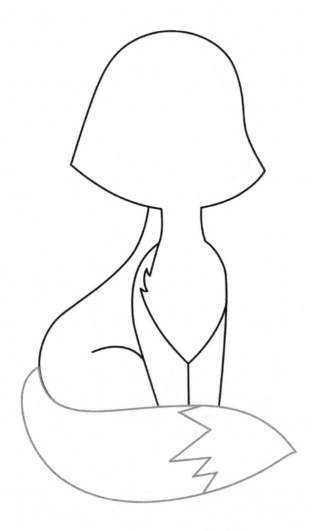

5) Add a big tail at the bottom of the body.

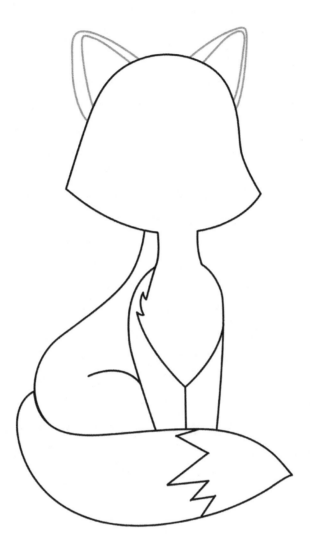

6) Add two sharp ears to the head.

7) Draw a line on the face in the area of the eyebrows and nose.

8) Add eyes, nose and mouth to face.

9) Done, let's start coloring!

10) Color picture using orange for body, pink for auricle, brown for paws, nose, ears and eyes, light yellow for face, tip of tail and belly.

11) Add some shadows and highlights to add volume.

12) Colored version.

How to draw Fox2

1) Draw a fox head just above the center of the leaf for a round top, pointed at the sides and slightly convex below.

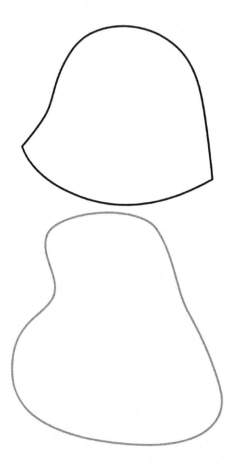

2) Draw a pear-shaped body.

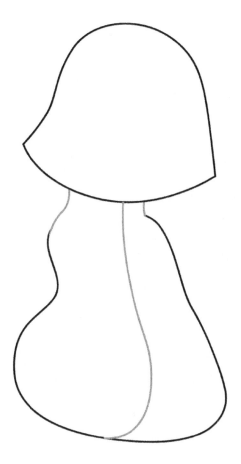

3) Add a couple of lines on the body for the neck and belly.

4) Draw the hind legs as shown in the example.

5) Draw the front paws, be close to the original.

6) Add a big tail at the bottom of the body.

7) Draw a line on the face in the area of the eyebrows and nose.

8) Add two sharp ears to the head.

9) Add eyes, nose and mouth to face.

10) Done, let's start coloring!

11) Color picture using orange for body, pink for auricle, brown for paws, nose, ears and eyes, light yellow for face, tip of tail and belly.

12) Add some shadows and highlights to add volume.

13) Colored version.

How to draw Fox3

1) Draw a fox head just above the center of the leaf for a round top, pointed at the sides and slightly convex below.

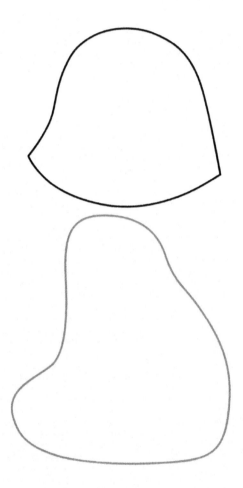

2) Draw a pear-shaped body.

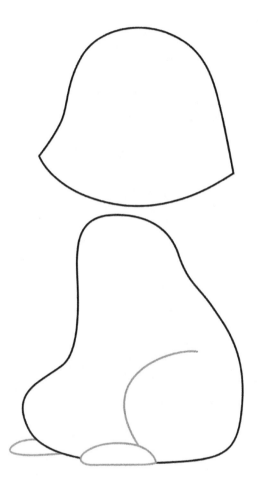

3) Add the hind legs, as shown in the example.

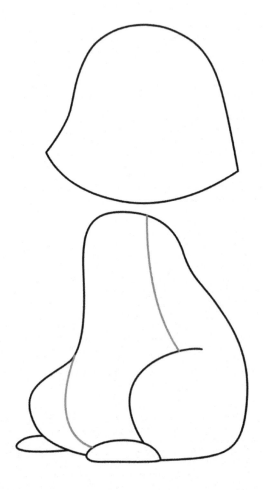

4) Add a couple of lines for the belly.

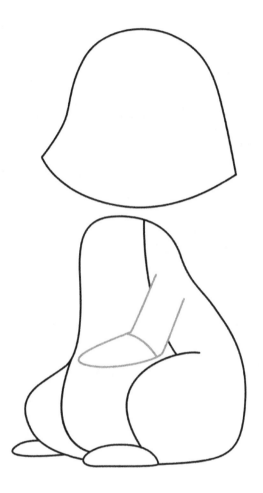

5) Draw one front paw.

6) Add a big tail at the bottom of the body.

7) Draw a scarf around the neck, be close to the original.

8) Draw a big cup of tea in the front paws.

9) Add two sharp ears to the head.

10) Draw a line on the face in the area of the eyebrows and nose.

11) Add eyes, nose and mouth to face.

12) Done, let's start coloring!

13) Color picture using orange for body, pink for auricle, brown for paws, nose, ears and eyes, light yellow for face, tip of tail and belly.

14) Add some shadows and highlights to add volume.

15) Colored version.

How to draw Fox4

1) Draw a fox head just above the center of the leaf for a round top, pointed at the sides and slightly convex below.

2) Draw a pear-shaped body.

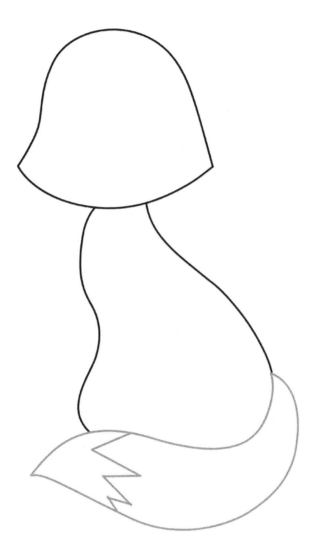

3) Add a big tail at the bottom of the body.

4) Add a couple of lines for the belly.

5) Draw the front paws.

6) Draw a book cover, be close to the original.

7) Draw pages inside the book.

8) Add two sharp ears to the head.

9) Draw a line on the face in the area of the eyebrows and nose.

10) Add eyes, nose and mouth to face.

11) Done, let's start coloring!

12) Color picture using orange for body, pink for auricle, brown for paws, nose, ears and eyes, light yellow for face, tip of tail and belly.

13) Add some shadows and highlights to add volume.

14) Colored version.

How to draw Fox5

1) Draw a fox head just above the center of the leaf for a round top, pointed at the sides and slightly convex below.

2) Draw a pear-shaped body.

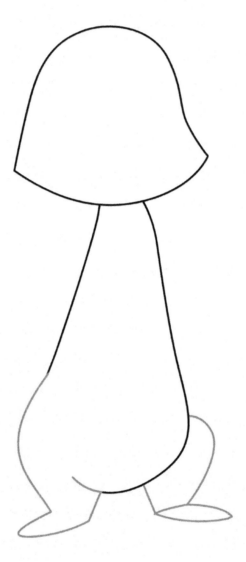

3) Add the hind legs, as shown in the example.

4) Draw the front paws, be close to the original.

5) Add a line for the belly.

6) Add a big tail at the bottom of the body.

7) Add two sharp ears to the head.

8) Draw a line on the face in the area of the eyebrows and nose.

9) Add eyes, nose and mouth to face.

10) Done, let's start coloring!

11) Color picture using orange for body, pink for auricle, brown for paws, nose, ears and eyes, light yellow for face, tip of tail and belly.

12) Add some shadows and highlights to add volume.

13) Colored version.

How to draw Fox6

1) Draw a little to the left of the center of the sheet for the head of the fox round on top, pointed at the sides and slightly convex below.

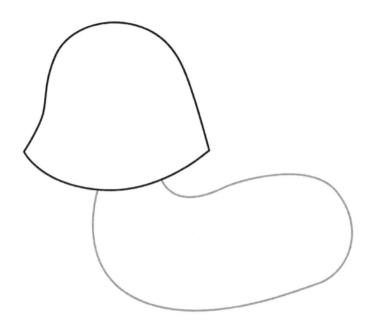

2) Draw a pear-shaped body.

3) Add the hind legs, as shown in the example.

4) Draw the front paws, be close to the original.

5) Add a line for the belly.

6) Add a big tail at the bottom of the body.

7) Add two sharp ears to the head.

8) Draw a line on the face in the area of the eyebrows and nose.

9) Add eyes, nose and mouth to face.

10) Done, let's start coloring!

11) Color picture using orange for body, pink for auricle, brown for paws, nose, ears and eyes, light yellow for face, tip of tail and belly.

12) Add some shadows and highlights to add volume.

13) Colored version.

How to draw Fox7

1) Draw a little to the left and below the center of the sheet for the head of a fox round on top, pointed at the sides and slightly convex at the bottom.

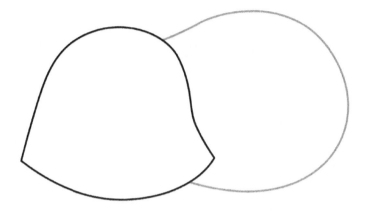

2) Draw a circle the size of the head a little behind it.

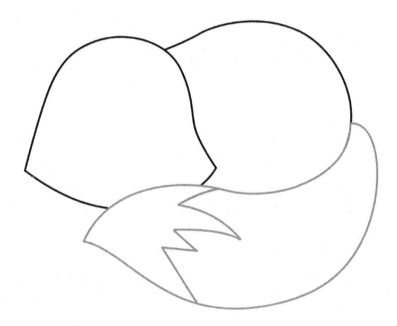

3) Add a big tail at the bottom of the body.

4) Add a pair of lines on the body for the rear legs.

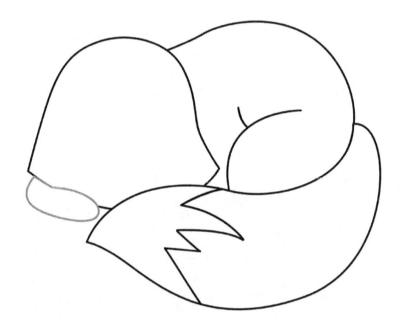

5) Draw the front paw under the head.

6) Add two sharp ears to the head.

7) Draw a line on the face in the area of the eyebrows and nose.

8) Add eyes, nose and mouth to face.

9) Done, let's start coloring!

10) Color picture using orange for body, pink for auricle, brown for paws, nose, ears and eyes, light yellow for face, tip of tail and belly.

11) Add some shadows and highlights to add volume.

12) Colored version.

About the Author

Kristen Diaz is an accomplished artist and e-book author living in Southern California. She has provided the illustrations for hundreds of children's books as her realistic and lifelike images appeal to children and adults alike.

Diaz began her career as an artist when she was in her 20's creating caricatures on the beaches of sunny California. What started as a way to make extra spending money turned into a successful career because of her amazing talent. Her comically accurate caricatures had a unique look and one of the local authors took notice. When the writer asked Diaz to illustrate one of her books, Kristen jumped at the opportunity to showcase her talent. The result was spectacular and soon Diaz was in high demand. Her ability to change her style to fit the books made her an attractive artist to work with.

She decided to get a more formal education in graphic design and illustration by enrolling in the Arts program at Platt's College which is where she met the love of her life and life partner, Terri. The two live in Pasadena close to the beach where Diaz' career first flourished. She occasionally hangs out on the beach with her easel and paints and makes caricatures of the humanity passing by. Her e-books are simple to follow and contain many witty anecdotes about her life in Pasadena.

Made in the USA
Coppell, TX
04 June 2021